FOLLOW THAT FOOD CHAIN

A DESERT Food Chain

A WHO-EATS-WHAT Adventure in North America

Rebecca Hogue Wojahn   Donald Wojahn

Lerner Publications Company
Minneapolis

For Eli and Cal. We hope this answers some of your questions.

There are many links in the chain that created this series. Thanks to Kristen McCurry Mohn, Carol Hinz, Kitty Creswell, Danielle Carnito, Sarah Olmanson, Paul Rodeen, the staff of the L. E. Phillips Memorial Public Library, and finally, Katherine Hogue

Lerner Publications Company
A division of Lerner Publishing Group, Inc.
241 First Avenue North
Minneapolis, MN 55401 U.S.A.

Website address: www.lernerbooks.com

Library of Congress Cataloging-in-Publication Data

Wojahn, Rebecca Hogue.
   A desert food chain : a who-eats-what adventure in North America / by Rebecca Hogue Wojahn and Donald Wojahn.
      p.   cm. — (Follow that food chain)
   Includes bibliographical references and index.
   ISBN 978–0–8225–7501–6 (lib. bdg. : alk. paper)
   1. Desert ecology—North America—Juvenile literature. 2. Food chains (Ecology)—North America—Juvenile literature. I. Wojahn, Donald.
II. Title.
QH541.5.D4W58 2009
577.54'16—dc22   2008027133

Manufactured in the United States of America
1 2 3 4 5 6 – BP – 14 13 12 11 10 09

Contents

Introduction
WELCOME TO THE SONORAN DESERT

As the sun goes down, the Sonoran Desert comes to life. All day, most of the animals shielded themselves from the broiling sun in tunnels, burrows, and dens. Some huddled in arroyos—streambeds that hold a smidge more shade than the rest of the desert. As the air temperature drops, the hot ground starts to cool. And the desert animals creep out to explore their prickly landscape of cactus and brush. Daytime flowers close their blooms, but nighttime flowers spread their petals to welcome visitors.

The Sonoran Desert gets just 4 to 8 inches (10 to 20 centimeters) of rain a year. It is one of the hardest places in the world to survive in. But despite the searing heat and the little rain, there's an amazing amount of life here. In this book, you'll meet just a few of the hardy creatures of the Sonoran Desert.

California

Arizona

UNITED STATES

The
Sonoran
Desert

5

MEXICO

A North American Desert

The Sonoran Desert is a large, hot desert in the southwestern United States and northwestern Mexico. Parts of Arizona and California are in the Sonoran Desert.

Choose a
TERTIARY CONSUMER

All the living things in the desert are necessary for its health and survival. From the coyote trotting across the crusty sand to the elf owl watching him from his hole in the saguaro cactus, the living things are all connected. Animals and other organisms feed on and transfer energy to one another. This is called a **food chain** or a **food web**.

In food chains, the strongest **predators** are called **tertiary consumers**. They hunt other animals for food and have few natural enemies. Some of the animals they eat are called **secondary consumers**. Secondary consumers are also predators. They hunt plant-eating animals. Plant eaters are **primary consumers**.

Plants are **producers**. Using energy from the sun, they produce their own food. Plants take in **nutrients** from the soil. They also provide nutrients to the animals that eat them.

Decomposers are insects or **bacteria** that break down dead plants and animals. Decomposers change them into the nutrients found in the soil.

The plants and animals in a food chain depend on one another. Sometimes there's a break in the chain, such as one type of animal dying out. This loss ripples through the rest of the **habitat**.

Begin your journey through the Sonoran Desert food web by choosing a powerful **carnivore**, or meat eater. These tertiary consumers are at the top of the food chain. That means that, for the most part, they don't have any enemies in the desert (except for humans).

When it's time for the tertiary consumer to eat, pick its meal and flip to that page. As you go through the book, don't be surprised if you backtrack and end up where you never expected to be. That's how food webs work—they're complicated. And watch out for those dead ends! When you hit one of those, you have to go back to page 7 and start over with another tertiary consumer.

6

The main role an animal plays in the desert food web is identified by a color-coded shape. Here is the key to that code:

TERTIARY CONSUMER

PRODUCER

SECONDARY CONSUMER

PRIMARY CONSUMER

DECOMPOSER

To choose . . .

. . . a coyote, TURN TO PAGE 8.
. . . a kit fox, TURN TO PAGE 20.
. . . an elf owl, TURN TO PAGE 36.
. . . an ocelot, TURN TO PAGE 54.

To learn more about a desert food web, GO TO PAGE 47.

COYOTE *(Canis latrans)*

As the moon rises over the horizon, a coyote tips his head back and lets out a long howl. In the distance, an echoing howl answers. The coyote sprays a little urine against a towering saguaro cactus and then jogs on. The scent he leaves behind lets other animals know that this is his territory.

He stops to sniff at some litter along the road. With a gulp, he swallows an old rotten sandwich. He's not picky about what he eats. Berries, bugs, garbage, or a fresh rabbit—he's learned to eat whatever he can find. It is because of this ability to **adapt** that there are more coyotes now than ever before. That kind of population growth doesn't happen very often in the wild.

In fact, there are so many coyotes that they are sometimes considered pests and are hunted and poisoned. But here, in the desert, they're a necessary part of the habitat. Mice and other rodents would soon clean the desert of all plants if coyotes weren't around to hunt them and keep their numbers down.

A coyote pup eats a rabbit.

Friend or Foe?

Coyotes often turn up in many old legends and folktales, particularly Native American ones. In the stories, the coyote is most often a trickster, someone who plays tricks on others and can't be trusted. Sometimes he is greedy, clever, and funny, while at other times he is a brave hero. People have a hard time deciding what to think about coyotes. Some want to protect them. Some want to hunt and poison them.

This coyote keeps hunting. The sandwich helped to fill him up, but he's hunting for his pups and their mom tonight too. He needs something he can bring back to the den for them. *Last night for dinner, he brought them . . .*

. . . **a baby kit fox hunting a little too far away from its mother.** To see what another kit fox is up to, TURN TO PAGE 20.

. . . **a dead Sonoran pronghorn.** To see what another Sonoran pronghorn is up to, TURN TO PAGE 35.

. . . **a desert tortoise pushing through the sand. Crunchy!** To see what another desert tortoise is up to, TURN TO PAGE 55.

. . . **Gila woodpecker eggs that fell out of the nest.** To see what another Gila woodpecker is up to, TURN TO PAGE 22.

. . . **a Merriam's kangaroo rat munching on seeds.** To see what another kangaroo rat is up to, TURN TO PAGE 50.

. . . **a collared peccary scratching in the dirt.** To see what another collared peccary is up to, TURN TO PAGE 44.

. . . **some short-horned grasshoppers.** To see what other short-horned grasshoppers are up to, TURN TO PAGE 30.

. . . **a pallid bat that swooped too low.** To see what another pallid bat is up to, TURN TO PAGE 38.

ROADRUNNER (*Geococcyx californianus*)

The roadrunner wakes with the sun. She fluffs up her tail feathers, turns her back to the sun, and lets her dark skin underneath soak up the warmth. It was chilly last night—almost freezing!

After warming up from the cold night, the roadrunner sets out for breakfast. She charges through the nearest group of bushes. With a whir and a buzz and a chirp, lizards, insects, and birds scatter out of her way. She stabs at a fleeing giant desert hairy scorpion but misses. Never mind, she'll just chase it down. She can run almost 20 miles (32 kilometers) per hour! She much prefers to run. Although her wings work, she flies for only a few feet at a time and only if something threatens her.

The roadrunner pauses next to some stones. Just then a rattlesnake gives a warning buzz behind her. Slowly, she turns to face it.

Desert Extremes

Roadrunners are built for the extreme conditions of the desert. Their bodies soak up any extra water from their waste before they poop it out. They get rid of salt through their noses. But it's not just the heat and dryness they've adapted to. At night, desert temperatures drop sharply. Roadrunners are able to lower their own body temperatures so it doesn't take as much energy to keep them warm. But then in the morning, roadrunners have to bring their temps back up quickly. So they often sun themselves to get revved up for the day.

Faster than you can blink, the roadrunner strikes at the rattlesnake. She pinches his tail in her beak. Before he can react, she cracks his body around like a whip. Keeping a tight grip on his tail, she slams his body on the ground over and over again. In less than a minute, he's her next meal. First, she stamps and pecks at his head to break up his skull bones—she doesn't have any teeth to chew him up. Then she swallows the first part of him—but he's too big for her to eat at one sitting. That's okay. She'll just let his tail hang out of her mouth for a few days until there's room in her stomach for the rest of him.

After she's eaten, she finds a quiet spot in the shade of a barrel cactus. The day is starting to really heat up. Instead of sunning to warm up, she starts panting to cool down. She settles in to enjoy another broiler of a day in the Sonoran Desert.

Last night for dinner, she beat up . . .

. . . **a short-horned grasshopper hiding under a leaf.** To see what another short-horned grasshopper is up to, TURN TO PAGE 30.

. . . **a pinacate beetle scuttling across the sand.** To see what another pinacate beetle is up to, TURN TO PAGE 52.

. . . **a cactus wren out hunting for food.** To see what another cactus wren is up to, TURN TO PAGE 48.

. . . **a Couch's spadefoot toad just breaking through the ground.** To see what another spadefoot toad is up to, TURN TO PAGE 24.

. . . **a chuckwalla basking in the sun.** To see what another chuckwalla is up to, TURN TO PAGE 14.

. . . **a giant desert hairy scorpion found under a rock.** To see what another scorpion is up to, TURN TO PAGE 16.

. . . **a western diamondback rattlesnake coiled under a bush.** To see what another diamondback rattlesnake is up to, TURN TO PAGE 26.

. . . **a desert centipede tucked under a log.** To see what another desert centipede is up to, TURN TO PAGE 42.

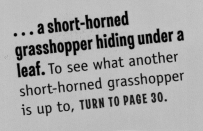

CHUCKWALLA
(*Sauromalus obesus*)

A chuckwalla basks in the sun on the edge of a rock. As a cold-blooded reptile, he can't control his body heat. His temperature changes with the weather. Last night's cold and rain made him stiff and slow this morning, even though he tried to stay warm by burrowing underground. A few hours in the sun should get his juices flowing.

But he doesn't relax for long. Something swoops by overhead. It's a hawk, scanning the desert below for an easy meal. The chuckwalla slides under the rock. He should be safe from the hawk here, but just in case, he starts gulping air. That saggy, baggy skin of his puffs out and fills up—just like a balloon. When he gulps air, he can suck in three hundred times more air than he can with a usual breath. Soon he has sucked in so much air that he is wedged tight between the stones. The tight fit and his rough skin make it nearly impossible for anyone to get him out. He'll deflate and come out only when he's ready. In the meantime, he'll wait.

Last night for dinner, the chuckwalla chomped . . .

Pet Trade

Despite their clever tricks against predators, chuckwallas are becoming scarce in the desert. More people in the desert means fewer places for chuckwallas to live. But another reason for their scarcity in the desert is that some people capture them to sell. People pay a lot of money to have a chuckwalla as a pet.

. . . a saguaro cactus. To see what a saguaro cactus is like, TURN TO PAGE 32.

. . . a Brady pincushion cactus. To see what a Brady pincushion cactus is like, TURN TO PAGE 19.

. . . creosote flowers—yum! Yellow food is his favorite. To see what desert flowers and trees are like, TURN TO PAGE 58.

GIANT DESERT HAIRY SCORPION
(*Hadrurus arizonensis*)

A scorpion crouches in a rock crack, waiting until it's dark enough to go out to hunt. Clinging to her back is a gang of tiny white scorpions—her babies. They'll hang there for about two weeks. Then they'll **molt** and get the hard **exoskeleton** that she has. Her back is probably the safest place for them—scorpion moms have been known to eat their own babies.

What's that? She senses something. The scorpion has many eyes, but she can't see well. Instead, the rough hairs on her body sense movements nearby. She holds tight until an unaware young kangaroo rat scurries closer. Closer . . . then—snap! Her giant pincers latch onto the rat and pin it in place. And—wham! Her tail whips over her head, spiking the rat with its deadly tip. **Venom** pulses into the rat's body.

16

A scorpion eats a beetle.

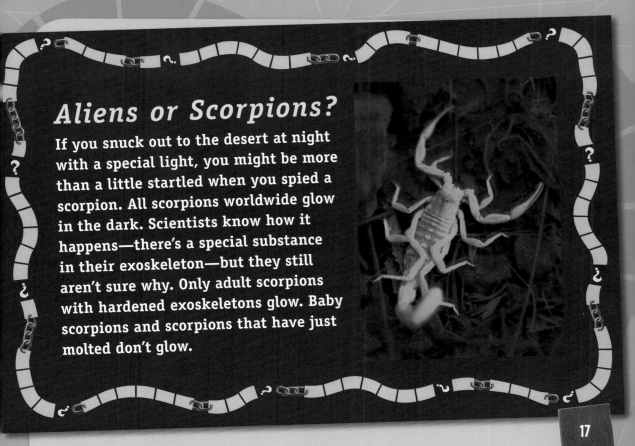

Aliens or Scorpions?

If you snuck out to the desert at night with a special light, you might be more than a little startled when you spied a scorpion. All scorpions worldwide glow in the dark. Scientists know how it happens—there's a special substance in their exoskeleton—but they still aren't sure why. Only adult scorpions with hardened exoskeletons glow. Baby scorpions and scorpions that have just molted don't glow.

In the scorpion's rush to down the baby rat, she's missed something. Circling overhead, someone else has spotted an easy meal. A barn owl swoops down and makes a grab for the struggling rat. The scorpion clings to her victim and is lifted high off the ground.

But the owl is either distracted or didn't get a good grip, because the still-twitching rat slips out of the owl's talons—and the scorpion along with it. They fall to the sand, the scorpion unhurt.

But it's too late for the rat. Within minutes, it is paralyzed from the scorpion's earlier sting. The scorpion untangles her eight legs and twelve body segments to get upright again. She crushes the rat with her larger pincers. Smaller pincers near her mouth tear the rat apart. Then she sucks down her **prey's** juices.

Scorpions don't need to eat every night. Once a month or so is fine for them. *Last month the scorpion ate for dinner . . .*

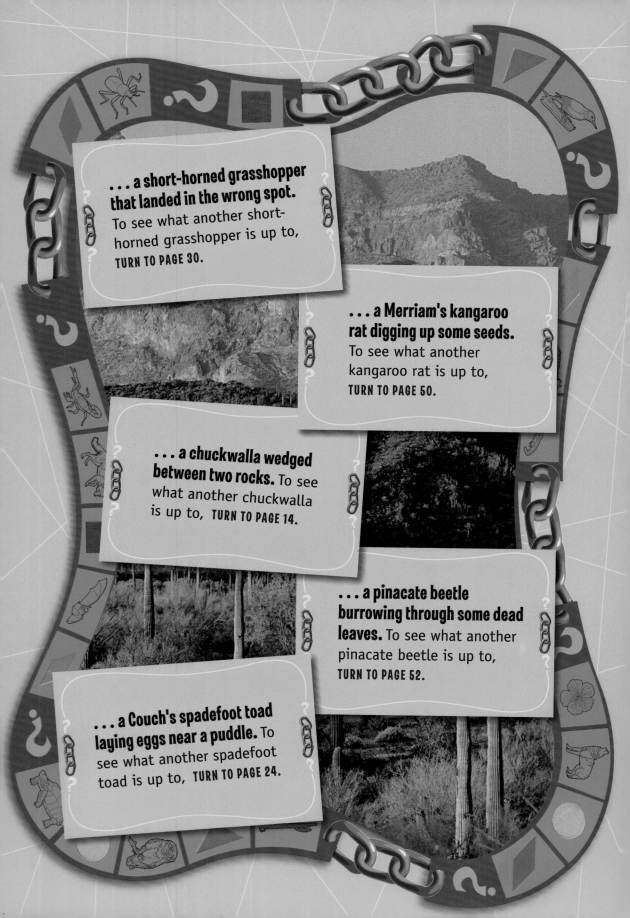

. . . a short-horned grasshopper that landed in the wrong spot. To see what another short-horned grasshopper is up to, TURN TO PAGE 30.

. . . a Merriam's kangaroo rat digging up some seeds. To see what another kangaroo rat is up to, TURN TO PAGE 50.

. . . a chuckwalla wedged between two rocks. To see what another chuckwalla is up to, TURN TO PAGE 14.

. . . a pinacate beetle burrowing through some dead leaves. To see what another pinacate beetle is up to, TURN TO PAGE 52.

. . . a Couch's spadefoot toad laying eggs near a puddle. To see what another spadefoot toad is up to, TURN TO PAGE 24.

BRADY PINCUSHION CACTUS
(*Pediocactus bradyi*)

Watch where you step! That tiny, spiny mound under the saguaro cactus has more than enough needles to make you sorry you stepped there. It's too bad all those spines on the Brady pincushion cactus can't protect it from other threats. That's right, this is a *DEAD END*. The Brady pincushion cactus is in danger of becoming **extinct**. More and more people are moving into the area. Hikers, cars, and all-terrain vehicles crush the soil and plants. People also bring pesticides—poisons to kill bugs and other pests—and these harm the cactuses. Laws have been passed against the use of pesticides near the cactuses. But when it rains, floodwaters can carry the poisons all over the desert.

KIT FOX (*Vulpes macrotis*)

an adult kit fox

A two-month-old kit fox peeks out of the den after her parents. Her huge ears twitch and turn at the night sounds. They've kept her cool all day—their size helps her body get rid of the heat—but for the first time, she'll use her ears for hunting. She cocks her head, listening for the *creak-creak-creak* of a cricket. When she's pinpointed it, she nabs it. It's the first meal she's caught all by herself.

There's a lot to learn in the desert night. She trots along after her parents. Although it cools off in the night, the sand is still very hot. Her hairy toes protect her feet. She watches as her mother pounces on a mouse. Then she follows as the catch is brought back to their den. There's no need to stop for a drink of water—kit foxes get all their water from their food.

Their den is a long burrow scratched out under the sand. It's the seventh one the kit fox has lived in so far. Anytime her parents get nervous, they move to a different den to protect their pups. Luckily, there are lots of old dens and burrows underground to pick from.

The kit fox squeezes her cat-sized body into the den's opening. She carefully avoids the piles of poop outside. Foxes always go outside so the den stays tidy. Inside it's cool and clean and lined with grass.

Even better—it's time to eat!

Last night for dinner, the kit fox family nibbled on . . .

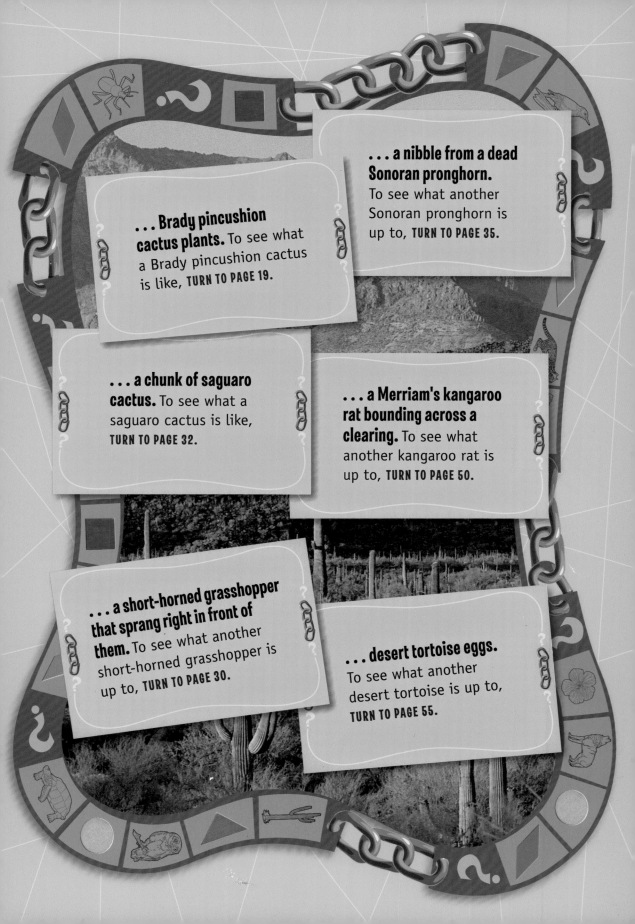

. . . **Brady pincushion cactus plants.** To see what a Brady pincushion cactus is like, TURN TO PAGE 19.

. . . **a nibble from a dead Sonoran pronghorn.** To see what another Sonoran pronghorn is up to, TURN TO PAGE 35.

. . . **a chunk of saguaro cactus.** To see what a saguaro cactus is like, TURN TO PAGE 32.

. . . **a Merriam's kangaroo rat bounding across a clearing.** To see what another kangaroo rat is up to, TURN TO PAGE 50.

. . . **a short-horned grasshopper that sprang right in front of them.** To see what another short-horned grasshopper is up to, TURN TO PAGE 30.

. . . **desert tortoise eggs.** To see what another desert tortoise is up to, TURN TO PAGE 55.

GILA WOODPECKER
(*Melanerpes uropygialis*)

Bam-bam-bam-bam-bam. A Gila woodpecker clings to the side of a saguaro cactus. He slams his beak into its tough skin over and over. He's clearing a nest for his family. You'd get a headache if you banged your face against something hard, but the woodpecker's body is made for it. He's got special muscles in his head that cushion the blows.

He's not hurting the cactus, either. In fact, the woodpecker is doing it a favor. The woodpecker family will gulp down all the pesky insects that could kill the cactus. In return, the cactus will provide the woodpecker with a safe home, high above the dangerous desert floor.

Pip! Pip! The woodpecker's mate, feeding on ants near the base of the plant, calls out a warning. An ocelot prowls through the mesquite trees and shrubs nearby.

The woodpecker pair fly off together. The nest hole is almost complete, but it'll still be a while before it's ready to live in. Once a hole is drilled in the cactus, the sap inside will need to dry out for several months before it can be used as a nest. They're done here for today.

Last night for dinner, the Gila woodpecker swallowed...

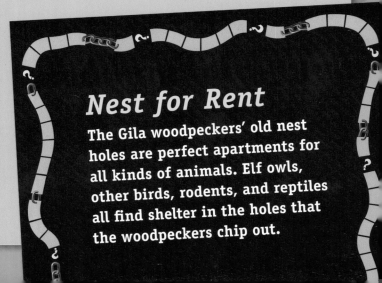

Nest for Rent

The Gila woodpeckers' old nest holes are perfect apartments for all kinds of animals. Elf owls, other birds, rodents, and reptiles all find shelter in the holes that the woodpeckers chip out.

. . . fruits, berries, and seeds from desert trees and flowers. To see what the desert trees and flowers are like, TURN TO PAGE 58.

. . . a short-horned grasshopper looking for a mate. To see what another short-horned grasshopper is up to, TURN TO PAGE 30.

. . . a baby chuckwalla just hatched from an egg. To see what another chuckwalla is up to, TURN TO PAGE 14.

. . . a pinacate beetle nibbling on a rotten agave. To see what another pinacate beetle is up to, TURN TO PAGE 52.

. . . a giant desert centipede that just left the safety of its mother. To see what another desert centipede is up to, TURN TO PAGE 42.

COUCH'S SPADEFOOT TOAD (*Scaphiopus couchii*)

A Couch's spadefoot toad scrapes the dirt aside as she makes her way up to the surface of the desert. She's spent almost eleven months huddled 3 feet (0.9 meters) underground in a cocoon made from the skin she shed. But last night's rain was a signal to come to the surface again. Toads need water to lay their eggs in, and the rain left behind lots of puddles.

But first she'll have to find a mate. As she breaks through the sandy crust, she's already listening for the croak of a male toad. She stretches her legs with a few hops. Then she hears it—a male spadefoot toad's cry. They meet in a muddy puddle under a sandy stone. He hops on her back, and she gives him a piggyback ride through the puddle. Behind them are shiny blobs of eggs.

Her work is finished, so she's free to eat. She leaps off into the brush, snagging insects with her tongue. She'll need to eat her fill—in just a few weeks, she'll head underground again.

Last night for dinner, the spadefoot toad didn't eat anything. She was still underground. *But the last time she did eat, she gobbled down . . .*

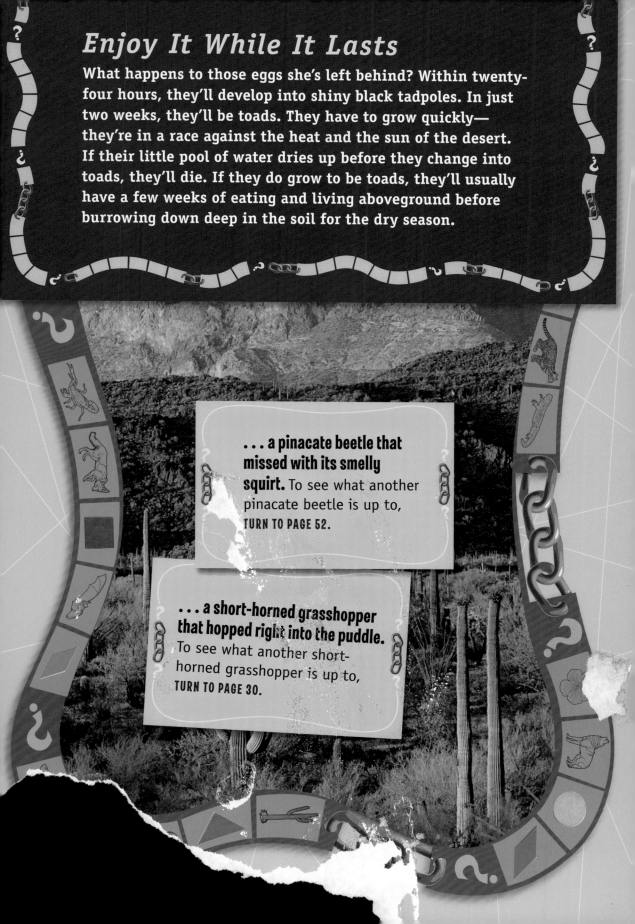

Enjoy It While It Lasts

What happens to those eggs she's left behind? Within twenty-four hours, they'll develop into shiny black tadpoles. In just two weeks, they'll be toads. They have to grow quickly—they're in a race against the heat and the sun of the desert. If their little pool of water dries up before they change into toads, they'll die. If they do grow to be toads, they'll usually have a few weeks of eating and living aboveground before burrowing down deep in the soil for the dry season.

. . . a pinacate beetle that missed with its smelly squirt. To see what another pinacate beetle is up to, TURN TO PAGE 52.

. . . a short-horned grasshopper that hopped right into the puddle. To see what another short-horned grasshopper is up to, TURN TO PAGE 30.

WESTERN DIAMONDBACK RATTLESNAKE
(*Crotalus atrox*)

A diamondback rattler coils up in a sunny spot under sagebrush. He's cold blooded, so he uses the sun's heat to warm up after a chilly night. But the day is getting too hot, so he moves into some shade.

Nearby, a peccary roots for food. The peccary, snuffling through the brush, doesn't notice the rattler. The crisscrossing pattern on the snake's back makes him hard to see in the speckled shadows on the sand. A few more steps and the peccary is too close. The rattler doesn't want to get stepped on.

He rears his head and shakes his tail. The rattles on the end of his tail buzz. He opens his mouth. His **venomous** fangs fold down. The peccary jumps—and gets the hint. She moves on, looking for food under a different bush.

Snake Medicine

Diamondback rattlesnakes use their venom to stun their prey. Then they swallow it whole. But the venom also helps break down the meal so the snake can digest it more easily.

You wouldn't think something so deadly could be helpful to people. But scientists are studying how rattlesnake venom might actually be used as a medicine for some human diseases and conditions. They are exploring the use of venom for paralyzed patients and for diseases such as Alzheimer's.

Instead of curling back up, the snake stretches out and slithers away. He's been feeling awfully tight and itchy lately. He rubs hard against the rough trunk of a blue paloverde tree. As he scrapes along, a tear in his skin opens up along his back.

He twists about the tree and slides along it in the other direction. Slowly, the split in his skin widens. As he twists and wiggles, the outer layer of his skin falls away behind him. His new skin underneath is shiny and bright—and one size larger.

The shed skin of a western diamondback rattlesnake

Along with his new skin, he's added a new rattle to his tail. Each time he sheds his skin, a rattle is added. It's somewhat true that you can tell a rattlesnake's age by its number of rattles. You can tell if it's an old snake or a young one. But since some snakes shed their skin several times in a year, counting the number of rattles won't tell you an exact age.

The snake winds away. His fresh new skin even gave his eyes a new layer. They're sensitive, and he can't see very well yet. He'll find a quiet spot to get used to them. Luckily, he ate well last night.

Last night for dinner, he gulped down . . .

. . . a roadrunner that tried to eat him. To see what another roadrunner is up to, TURN TO PAGE 11.

. . . a giant desert hairy scorpion laying her eggs. To see what another scorpion is up to, TURN TO PAGE 16.

. . . a desert tortoise just coming out of its den. To see what another desert tortoise is up to, TURN TO PAGE 55.

. . . a baby collared peccary that roamed too far from its mother. To see what another collared peccary is up to, TURN TO PAGE 44.

. . . a cactus wren hunting on the ground. To see what another cactus wren is up to, TURN TO PAGE 48.

. . . a Merriam's kangaroo rat digging up seeds. To see what another kangaroo rat is up to, TURN TO PAGE 50.

. . . a Gila woodpecker pounding away at the bottom of a cactus. To see what another Gila woodpecker is up to, TURN TO PAGE 22.

. . . an elf owl hunting food for his family. To see what another elf owl is up to, TURN TO PAGE 36.

SHORT-HORNED GRASSHOPPER
(*Valanga nigricornis*)

A short-horned grasshopper pulls his back wing against a vein in his front wing. A scratchy hum starts, growing louder and louder. It's a huge noise from something the size of a paper clip!

In a moment, more grasshoppers in the creosote bush echo back. Other males are warning him off, while the females are asking him to come find them. The grasshopper doesn't have ears. He hears their voices with the flat spots on the sides of his head, called tympana. He's not interested in a mate now. He just needs some space. He pushes off with his powerful back legs and lands on an empty branch above.

Creosote leaves are his favorite, but he's not all that hungry. Instead of eating, he takes tiny gulps of air. This fills him up and presses his insides tight against his hard **exoskeleton**. Soon a crack appears along his back. As it falls away, he steps out wearing his new skin and unfolds even bigger wings. And that means even louder grasshopper music!

Last night for dinner, the grasshopper munched on . . .

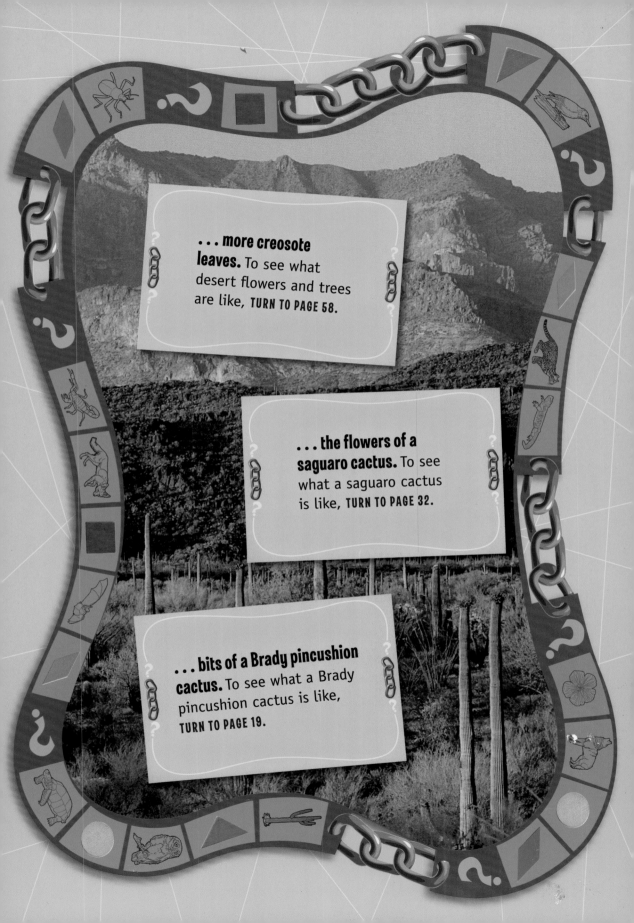

. . . more creosote leaves. To see what desert flowers and trees are like, TURN TO PAGE 58.

. . . the flowers of a saguaro cactus. To see what a saguaro cactus is like, TURN TO PAGE 32.

. . . bits of a Brady pincushion cactus. To see what a Brady pincushion cactus is like, TURN TO PAGE 19.

SAGUARO CACTUS (*Carnegiea gigantea*)

Thunder cracks and rain pours over a saguaro cactus. This may be the only water it gets for a year. The saguaro cactus drinks it up with roots just under the surface of the desert. The water travels up the cactus. Its trunk is pleated like a paper fan. As the cactus fills with water, the folds smooth out. Before the night is over, the cactus will be twice as wide as it was yesterday. This three-story-high giant holds over 200 gallons (760 liters) of water—and it'll live off all of it throughout the hot, dry days.

This saguaro cactus wasn't always the king of the desert. Two hundred years ago, it started as a tiny seed the size of a period. It grew in the shade of a "nurse" tree—a mesquite tree that sheltered it. After twenty-five years, the cactus was just 1 foot (0.3 meters) tall. When it was fifty years old, a moth visited its very first bloom. A cactus wren built a nest on its first arm when it was seventy-five years old. As the years passed, the saguaro stretched and grew, adding arms and providing food and shelter for hundreds of desert animals.

Last night for dinner, the saguaro cactus soaked up the sun, drank up some water, breathed in carbon dioxide from the air, and absorbed nutrients from the soil from...

This saguaro cactus is home to a hawk family.

Stop Thief!

Despite being protected by law, saguaro cactuses are disappearing from the desert. Believe it or not, they're being stolen. It has become trendy for people in the southwestern United States to have a saguaro cactus in their yard. So cactus thieves sneak into the desert and dig up the saguaros to sell for hundreds of dollars. The thieves don't seem to be considering how long it'll take the desert to replace a lost saguaro—a hundred years or more. Meanwhile, what happens to all the creatures that depend on that cactus for food and shelter?

33

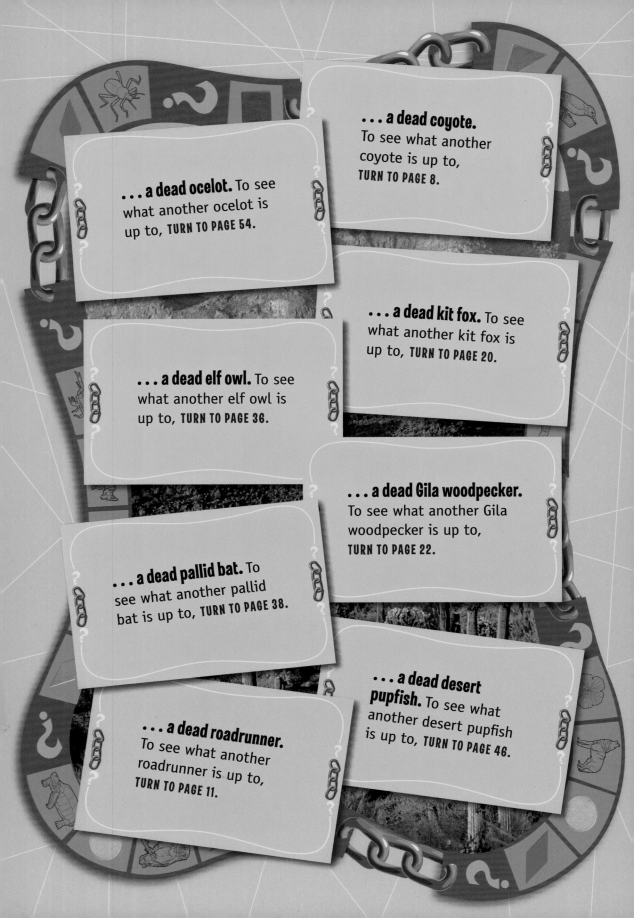

. . . **a dead ocelot.** To see what another ocelot is up to, TURN TO PAGE 54.

. . . **a dead coyote.** To see what another coyote is up to, TURN TO PAGE 8.

. . . **a dead kit fox.** To see what another kit fox is up to, TURN TO PAGE 20.

. . . **a dead elf owl.** To see what another elf owl is up to, TURN TO PAGE 36.

. . . **a dead Gila woodpecker.** To see what another Gila woodpecker is up to, TURN TO PAGE 22.

. . . **a dead pallid bat.** To see what another pallid bat is up to, TURN TO PAGE 38.

. . . **a dead desert pupfish.** To see what another desert pupfish is up to, TURN TO PAGE 46.

. . . **a dead roadrunner.** To see what another roadrunner is up to, TURN TO PAGE 11.

SONORAN PRONGHORN
(Antilocarpa americana sonoriensis)

The Sonoran pronghorn licks her baby, called a kid. She cleans him of all smells so predators can't find him. She tucks him in his hiding spot. She joins the rest of the herd, grazing on prickly pears and desert grasses farther down the canyon.

As the night grows darker, the kid waits for his mother. But his mother never returns for him.

That's why this is a *DEAD END*. This little kid is one out of just one hundred Sonoran pronghorns left in the wild in the United States. Pronghorns don't jump, so as new fences, roads, and buildings are developed, it gets harder for pronghorns to roam and look for food.

A car might have hit his mother. There's so much more traffic through the desert these days, especially with the new housing developments being built. Or maybe an old-fashioned predator, such as a coyote or a mountain lion, got her. Either way, the little pronghorn kid has a very slim chance of surviving without a mom to look after him.

An adult male Sonoran pronghorn

Sun Signal

Do you see that blaze of white in the distance? A pronghorn doe is flashing the "sun signal." The long white hairs on her rear are raised up, creating a bright, round flare that sends a warning across the desert: *Danger coming!* The rest of her herd echoes the signal and flees. The herd pounds out of the canyon at 60 miles (97 kilometers) per hour—the top speed of any North American animal!

ELF OWL *(Micrathene whitneyi)*

Churr, churr. The elf owl babies beg for food. Their mother stands guard over their nest which is safely tucked in an old Gila woodpecker's hole at the top of a saguaro cactus.

The father elf owl flies over to the nest. He looks more like a huge moth than an owl. He's just 5 inches (13 cm) long—not much bigger than your hand. He perches on the lip of the dried-out hole in the cactus with a spider clenched in his hooked beak. The babies inside open wide as their mother takes the spider. Each chick has a white "moustache" marking above its mouth to help her aim. She picks one chick and tucks the spider in.

The dad flaps off again. Unlike most owls, his flight isn't silent. Elf owls don't have soft wing tips like other owls. He skims the ground for a giant desert hairy scorpion, snatching it up in his tiny talons. He returns to the nest. Hunting will keep him busy tonight. He'll bring his family something new to eat almost every minute all night long.
Last night for dinner, the elf owl family munched on . . .

. . . **a desert pupfish scooped from his muddy puddle.** To see what another desert pupfish is up to, TURN TO PAGE 46.

. . . **a giant desert hairy scorpion just coming out for the evening.** To see what another scorpion is up to, TURN TO PAGE 16.

. . . **a western diamondback rattler hatchling.** To see what another diamondback rattler is up to, TURN TO PAGE 26.

. . . **a giant desert centipede curled around her eggs.** To see what another desert centipede is up to, TURN TO PAGE 42.

. . . **a short-horned grasshopper resting on the cactus.** To see what another short-horned grasshopper is up to, TURN TO PAGE 30.

. . . **a pallid bat that had just pounced on a scorpion.** To see what another pallid bat is up to, TURN TO PAGE 38.

. . . **a Merriam's kangaroo rat sniffing near a paloverde tree.** To see what another kangaroo rat is up to, TURN TO PAGE 50.

PALLID BAT (*Antrozous pallidus*)

The pallid bat opens her eyes and unfolds her wings. She's hanging upside down in a tight crack in a canyon. Around her, the colony of bat mothers and babies is stirring. It's been dark for about an hour. It's time for the moms to starting hunting. The bat uses the hooks on the tops of her wings to creep to the opening. She passes her nearly hairless twin babies on the way out. They'll hang tight on the rock until she returns in the morning.

Outside, the air is much cooler. She mingles with the other pallid bats—including the males, who are just sneaking out of their daytime roost. She flaps her blonde wings, looping up and down about 5 feet (1.5 meters) over the desert. Her huge ears are tuned in to the creatures of the night on the desert floor below.

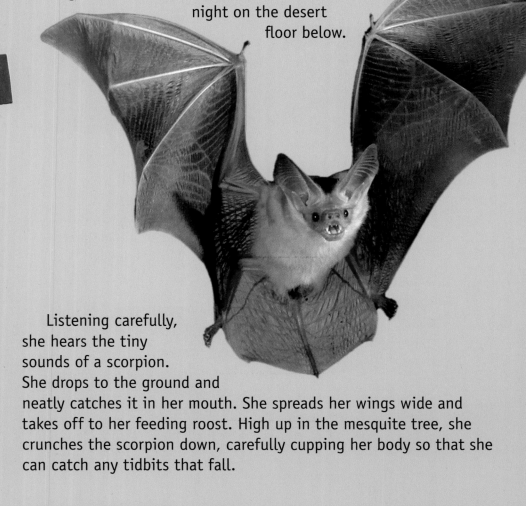

Listening carefully, she hears the tiny sounds of a scorpion. She drops to the ground and neatly catches it in her mouth. She spreads her wings wide and takes off to her feeding roost. High up in the mesquite tree, she crunches the scorpion down, carefully cupping her body so that she can catch any tidbits that fall.

A pallid bat eats its catch—a scorpion.

Ground Hunters

The pallid bat is one of a kind in how it hunts on the ground. Most bats that eat insects catch them in midair, using echolocation. As they fly, they send out a high-pitched sound (so high humans can't hear it). The sound bounces off objects and sends an echo back to the bat. Echolocation is so exact that it tells the bat the size, shape, distance, and direction of its prey. Pallid bats use echolocation too, but usually they nab their food on the ground.

The bat flaps back to the ground for a centipede. But just as she lands, a coyote bounds out from behind a cholla cactus—straight for her!

Forget about that centipede. If she doesn't get out of here, she's going to be the coyote's next meal! She takes off into the air just as the coyote pounces. His claws hook her right wing. She tumbles a little but manages to get out of reach. Still, she's badly injured. She hobbles to her feeding roost. A skunklike smell hangs around her. She releases it when she's in danger.

Even though she's hurt, she has to keep hunting. She needs to eat her body weight in insects tonight so that she'll make enough milk to feed her babies. If she quits, all three of them will die.

She tries out the wing once more and lifts into flight. This time she manages to catch a scorpion and bring it back to her feeding roost.

Luckily, the rest of the night is much less eventful. As day breaks, the pallid bats around her start squeaking. The colony takes off together, swooping through the early morning sky—the males to their daytime roost and the mothers back to their babies in their roosts.

Last night for dinner, the bat hunted . . .

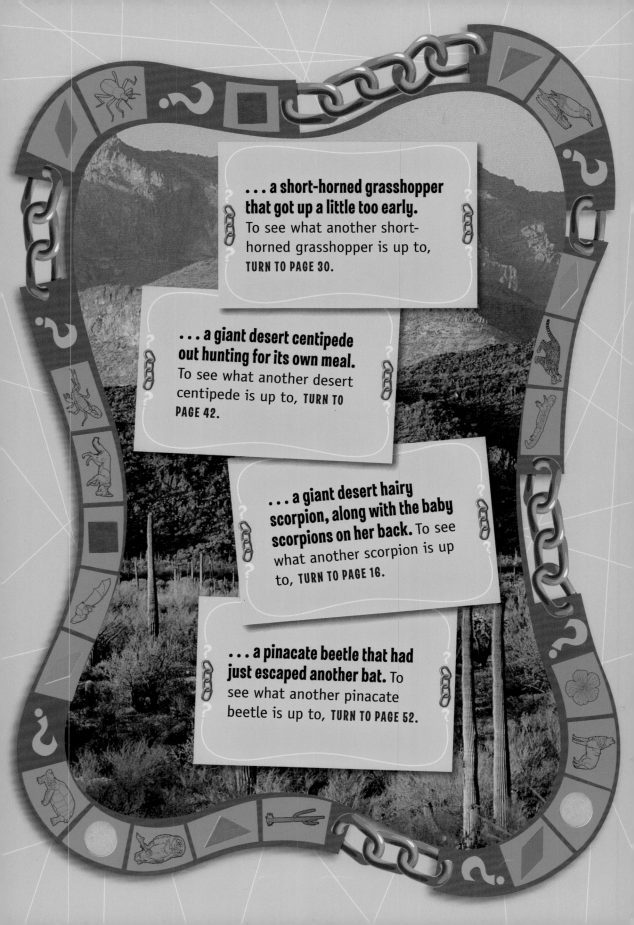

. . . a short-horned grasshopper that got up a little too early. To see what another short-horned grasshopper is up to, TURN TO PAGE 30.

. . . a giant desert centipede out hunting for its own meal. To see what another desert centipede is up to, TURN TO PAGE 42.

. . . a giant desert hairy scorpion, along with the baby scorpions on her back. To see what another scorpion is up to, TURN TO PAGE 16.

. . . a pinacate beetle that had just escaped another bat. To see what another pinacate beetle is up to, TURN TO PAGE 52.

GIANT DESERT CENTIPEDE *(Scolopendra heros)*

A giant desert centipede lays her last egg. She bundles the sticky batch of forty eggs together. She wraps every segment of her long orange body and every pair of legs around them. She's as long as a man's shoe and has more than forty pairs of legs!

Over the next few days, she grooms and tends her eggs. She makes sure no mold or germs are growing on them. When the babies hatch, they will be white, with only six or seven pairs of legs. And they'll be helpless. After a few days and a few **molts**—with another pair of legs added each time—they'll wander off on their own. Then the mother will be back to searching the desert at night and sucking down the insects and creatures she finds.

Even as adults, centipedes have to be careful to come out only at night. Their **exoskeletons** don't have the waxy coating that other desert animals have, so they dry out very easily. That's why you'll only find them in the darkest, most hidden places of the desert. Be careful turning over those rocks!

Last night for dinner, the centipede stuck her pincers into . . .

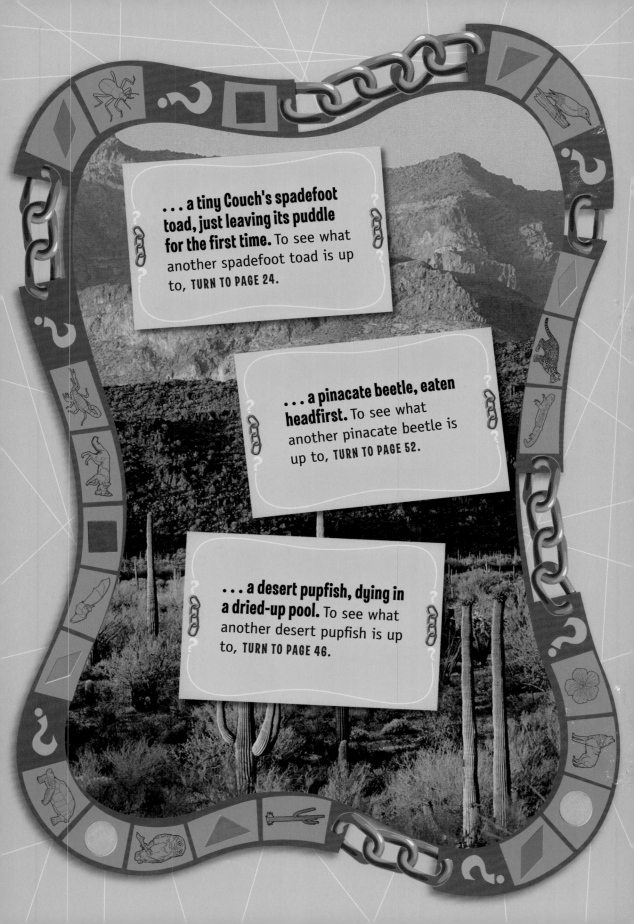

. . . a tiny Couch's spadefoot toad, just leaving its puddle for the first time. To see what another spadefoot toad is up to, TURN TO PAGE 24.

. . . a pinacate beetle, eaten headfirst. To see what another pinacate beetle is up to, TURN TO PAGE 52.

. . . a desert pupfish, dying in a dried-up pool. To see what another desert pupfish is up to, TURN TO PAGE 46.

COLLARED PECCARY
(Tayassu tajacu)

A collared peccary extends his oversized head and leans his long snout toward his cousin's. Avoiding each other's sharp tusks, he rubs his face on hers. Oil from the scent gland near his eye is spread on her. Even though the odor is very strong, she doesn't seem to mind. The smell means she's one of the herd.

As the herd snacks on agaves and prickly pears, he wanders off to rub his scent on a few stones. As the leader of this herd of fifteen peccaries, it's his job to mark their territory with his scent.

Suddenly, there's barking in the distance. A stray dog rushes at a young peccary on the outskirts of the herd. The dog barks and charges, nipping at the peccary. With a few coughlike grunts, the entire herd charges the dog.

With all those sharp tusks coming at him, the dog quickly scoots off, back toward home. He's lucky. Peccaries won't fight unless attacked. But if a dog starts a fight with a peccary, the dog usually loses.

The herd settles down. It's getting dark, so they huddle together for warmth as the heat of the desert fades away.

Last night for dinner, the peccaries downed . . .

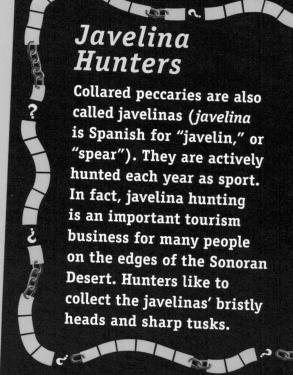

Javelina Hunters

Collared peccaries are also called javelinas (*javelina* is Spanish for "javelin," or "spear"). They are actively hunted each year as sport. In fact, javelina hunting is an important tourism business for many people on the edges of the Sonoran Desert. Hunters like to collect the javelinas' bristly heads and sharp tusks.

. . . a Brady pincushion cactus. To see what a Brady pincushion cactus is like, TURN TO PAGE 19.

. . . a young saguaro cactus. To see what a saguaro cactus is like, TURN TO PAGE 32.

. . . more fruit from desert trees and flowers. To see what desert flowers and trees are like, TURN TO PAGE 58.

. . . a giant desert centipede found curled up under some leaves. To see what another giant desert centipede is up to, TURN TO PAGE 42.

. . . a baby western diamondback rattlesnake. To see what another diamondback rattlesnake is up to, TURN TO PAGE 26.

DESERT PUPFISH (*Cyprinodon macularius*)

A fish in the desert? Maybe it won't surprise you that this is a **DEAD END**. But desert pupfish weren't always so rare. These algae eaters used to splash in the pools, springs, and streams of the desert. They burrowed deep in the mud to stay warm in the winter. In the summer, hot temperatures dried up many puddles, but pupfish stayed alive by crowding into the few remaining wet spots. But with more people living in the desert, there's just not room for these tiny silver fish. Even more troublesome is the arrival of **invasive species** of fish. People have released fish that don't grow naturally in the desert—sometimes these fish are old pets. These newcomers have eaten up and pushed out the desert pupfish.

A DESERT FOOD WEB

In the desert, energy moves around the food chain from the sun to plants, from plants to plant eaters, and from animals to the creatures that eat them. Energy also moves from dead animals to the plants and animals that draw nutrients from them.

CACTUS WREN (*Campylorhynchus brunneicapillus*)

The male cactus wren pinches a bit of dried grass in his sharp, pointed beak. He tucks it into the nest he's building between the spines of a cholla cactus. It's almost done.

He's getting better with practice. This is the third nest he's made this spring. Hopefully, this one will convince the female cactus wren to be his mate.

She flits over and peers in the dark entrance. Finally—she hops in! He follows. Together, they line the inside with feathers.

But—*crackle, crunch*—their work is interrupted. The male peeks out. A squirrel stuffs seeds in his cheeks and rummages around outside of the nest. The wrens streak out of the nest to protect the male's hard work. *Peck! Peck!* With their pointy beaks, they hammer at the squirrel. He squeaks and drops the seeds. As he races down the cholla, they chase him, pecking, poking, and shrieking. Finally, the squirrel scampers off to find an easier place to dine.

The wren couple return to their nest. They need to prepare for the eggs that will fill it soon.

Last night for dinner, the wren pecked ...

Birds with Attitude

Most wrens are shy and fearful. Not cactus wrens. They are nosy and pushy. They forcefully protect their nests. If another bird makes a nest nearby, they'll go out of their way to get rid of it. They'll peck and push the eggs right out of the nest and then pull the whole thing apart.

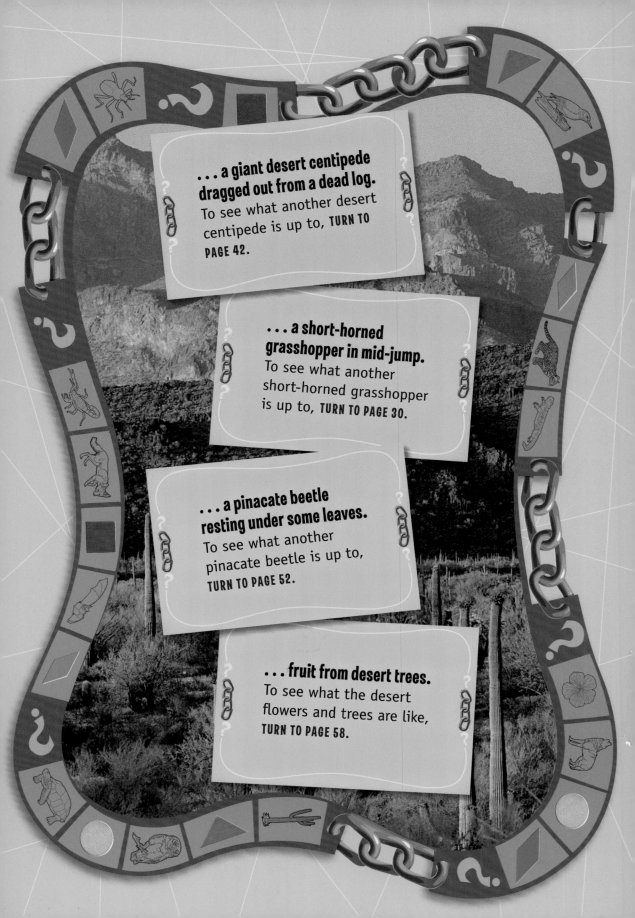

. . . a giant desert centipede dragged out from a dead log.
To see what another desert centipede is up to, TURN TO PAGE 42.

. . . a short-horned grasshopper in mid-jump.
To see what another short-horned grasshopper is up to, TURN TO PAGE 30.

. . . a pinacate beetle resting under some leaves.
To see what another pinacate beetle is up to, TURN TO PAGE 52.

. . . fruit from desert trees.
To see what the desert flowers and trees are like, TURN TO PAGE 58.

MERRIAM'S KANGAROO RAT
(Dipodomys merriami)

The kangaroo rat pushes off with his huge hind feet and legs and leaps through the air. No wonder he's called a kangaroo rat. He's less than a foot (0.3 meter) long, including his tail, but the back part of him looks and moves just like a tiny version of an Australian kangaroo.

At the base of an ocotillo plant, he burrows in the ground. Ah, there it is—a secret stash of seeds, buried a few weeks ago. He has treasures like these hidden all over his territory.

The rat nibbles at the seeds. They're the only food he lives on—he doesn't even drink water. He is so well **adapted** to the desert's dryness that his body converts the seeds he eats into water. As the seeds move through his system, the water is all used up. Even when he urinates, there's no liquid—just tiny pebbles of urine. To help conserve water, he only goes out at night. That way he avoids the drying heat of the sun.

Morning is coming, so the kangaroo rat heads underground. It's cooler down there, and the air has a little more moisture. He takes one last swallow and leaps off to his burrow.

Last night for dinner, the kangaroo rat nibbled on . . .

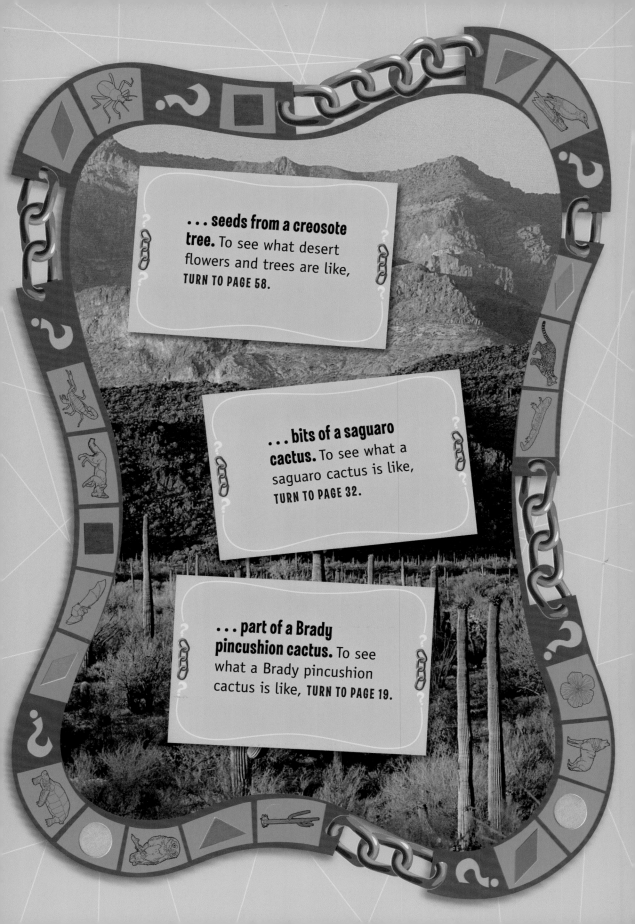

. . . **seeds from a creosote tree.** To see what desert flowers and trees are like, TURN TO PAGE 58.

. . . **bits of a saguaro cactus.** To see what a saguaro cactus is like, TURN TO PAGE 32.

. . . **part of a Brady pincushion cactus.** To see what a Brady pincushion cactus is like, TURN TO PAGE 19.

PINACATE BEETLE (*Eleodes armata*)

A pinacate beetle zigzags across the sand, his head low and his rear end pushed up high. His long black antennas stretch ahead of him, seeking out food. Tiny wings are tucked under his hard black shell, but they aren't nearly strong enough for flying. So he walks. Up and over the sand and stones, he hunts. Dead plants are a favorite of this decomposer, so he's also providing a nice service as he eats— desert cleanup duty.

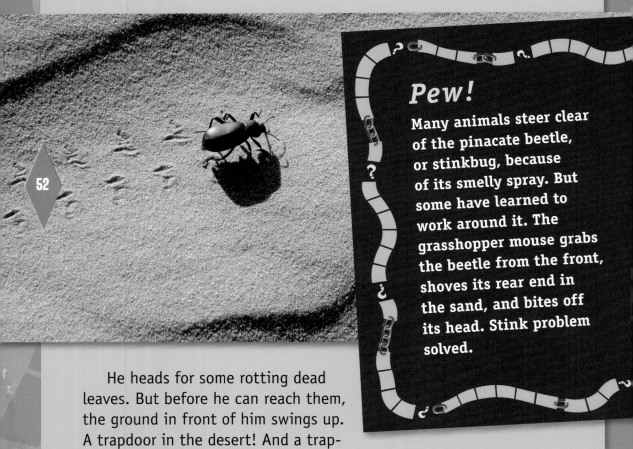

52

Pew!

Many animals steer clear of the pinacate beetle, or stinkbug, because of its smelly spray. But some have learned to work around it. The grasshopper mouse grabs the beetle from the front, shoves its rear end in the sand, and bites off its head. Stink problem solved.

He heads for some rotting dead leaves. But before he can reach them, the ground in front of him swings up. A trapdoor in the desert! And a trapdoor spider is behind it. But the pinacate beetle is ready. He raises his backside and aims. Squirt! He sprays a reddish brown substance at the spider. The spray stings and stinks and sticks. By the time the spider recovers, the pinacate beetle has wandered off with its rear end in the ready position.

Last night for dinner, the pinacate beetle ate . . .

. . . bits off a dead saguaro cactus. To see what a saguaro cactus is like, TURN TO PAGE 32.

. . . a Brady pincushion cactus. To see what a Brady pincushion cactus is like, TURN TO PAGE 19.

. . . dead leaves from a soaptree yucca. To see what the desert flowers and trees are like, TURN TO PAGE 58.

. . . a dead western diamondback rattlesnake. To see what another rattlesnake is up to, TURN TO PAGE 26.

. . . a dead kit fox. To see what another kit fox is up to, TURN TO PAGE 20.

OCELOT (*Leopardus pardalis*)

The ocelot stalks through the canyon. He's traveled almost 5 miles (8 kilometers) tonight, hunting down a kangaroo rat and a rabbit. With a full tummy, he's roaming in search of a female ocelot.

Ree-ow. He calls again. He's been looking for weeks, but he may never find a mate. Ocelots are becoming rare around the Sonoran Desert. In fact, fewer than one hundred are left in the United States. Many people are worried that ocelots may soon become **extinct**. And that makes this a *DEAD END*.

For years, ocelots were hunted and trapped. It's very hard for the ocelot population to increase. Ocelots have few babies, the babies take a long time to grow, and they have a high chance of dying young. Even though current laws protect ocelots, it may be too late.

54

Connect and Protect

The ocelots left in the Sonoran Desert are stranded in small sections of land. This makes it hard for them to find a mate and for new families to begin. But recently, several environmental organizations from the United States and Mexico have joined together to see if they can help. They are creating a protected corridor, or route, between the ocelots in the United States and those in Mexico. That way the two groups can get together, mate, and have more babies.

DESERT TORTOISE *(Gopherus agassizii)*

A desert tortoise pushes her stumpy shovel-like feet into the soil and plows across the sand. Slow but steady, she makes her way to the hole she's dug at the bottom of a small hill. The little bit of rain from the night before might have collected in the hole.

Ah, yes! She sips a bit. She can finally urinate. She's been saving every bit of water in her body for months—including her urine. After relieving herself, she drinks her fill. She'll store this new water in her body so that she can live through another long dry spell.

A desert tortoise emerges from its burrow.

Suddenly, yips and barks fill the air. The tortoise freezes. She watches as two playful coyote pups tumble down the side of the hill. One sniffs the tortoise. The other bats her with his paw. Uh-oh. The tortoise yanks her head and legs inside her shell. Luckily, her shell has hardened. During the first six years of her life, her shell was only the thickness of a human fingernail. This made her easy **prey**. In fact, many of her brothers and sisters didn't survive to adulthood.

A swat from one of the pups flips the tortoise over on her back. The pups spin her around a few times, but then their mother calls and they trot away. But the tortoise is still in danger. If she can't flip herself back over, she'll die.

The tortoise twists and rocks. She uses the uneven ground to get herself back on her feet. Whew!

She plods on. After a few bites of a beavertail cactus, she scoots to her burrow underground. She slides into the ancient hole. As she settles in, the ground above her begins to rumble. Sand shakes down on her head. Then it fades away. Even though her burrow has been used by generations of tortoises for thousands of years, the all-terrain vehicles cruising through the desert above her can cause it to collapse in an instant.

56

Last night for dinner, the tortoise crunched . . .

Tortoises in Trouble

Desert tortoises aren't technically endangered yet, but they're close. As more people creep into the desert on foot, by car, and on ATVs, the tortoise burrows are destroyed. Tortoises are also at risk because of invasive species of plants—plants that don't grow naturally in the desert. These plants tend to take over, and the tortoises' favorite foods don't grow anymore. Finally, people use the desert as a garbage dump. The trash draws lots of ravens—birds that love to snack on baby tortoises.

. . . a saguaro cactus. To see what a saguaro cactus is like, TURN TO PAGE 32.

. . . desert flowers. To see what the desert flowers and trees are like, TURN TO PAGE 58.

. . . a short-horned grasshopper that was missing a wing. To see what another short-horned grasshopper is up to, TURN TO PAGE 30.

. . . a giant desert centipede found under a rock. To see what another desert centipede is up to, TURN TO PAGE 42.

. . . a Brady pincushion cactus. To see what another Brady pincushion cactus is up to, TURN TO PAGE 19.

. . . a pinacate beetle trapped in some leaves the tortoise ate. To see what another pinacate beetle is up to, TURN TO PAGE 52.

DESERT TREES AND FLOWERS

Yesterday, the desert was a brown, crunchy place. After last night's rains, mariposa lilies, Mexican gold poppies, and daisies carpet the desert in color. The ocotillo bushes pop their tiny leaves out again, while the mesquite and paloverde trees' long taproots slurp up the moisture deep underground. All desert plants have to work fast to make the most of the water when it comes, so they burst into bloom in a rainbow of color.

Their blooms draw in bees, butterflies, bats, mice, and more. All this buzzing around the flowers **pollinates** them. Then the plants can produce the fruit and seeds that will help make sure they'll be around next year. As producers in the desert food web, it's very important that they survive. Without them, the food web would fall apart.

Within weeks the plants begin to fade as the scorching heat saps their moisture. Soon their seeds spill onto the desert floor. Then animals go to work. Birds scratch in the soil looking for insects—and unknowingly plant the seeds. Squirrels and mice carry seeds away and bury them in new places where they'll sprout next year.

Last night for dinner, the desert plants soaked up the sun, drank up some water, breathed in carbon dioxide from the air, and absorbed nutrients from the soil from ...

Above: An ocotillo in bloom
Below: Mexican gold poppies

sunlight

oxygen

carbon dioxide

Plants make food and oxygen through photosynthesis. Plants draw in carbon dioxide (a gas found in air) and water. Then they use the energy from sunlight to turn the carbon dioxide and water into their food.

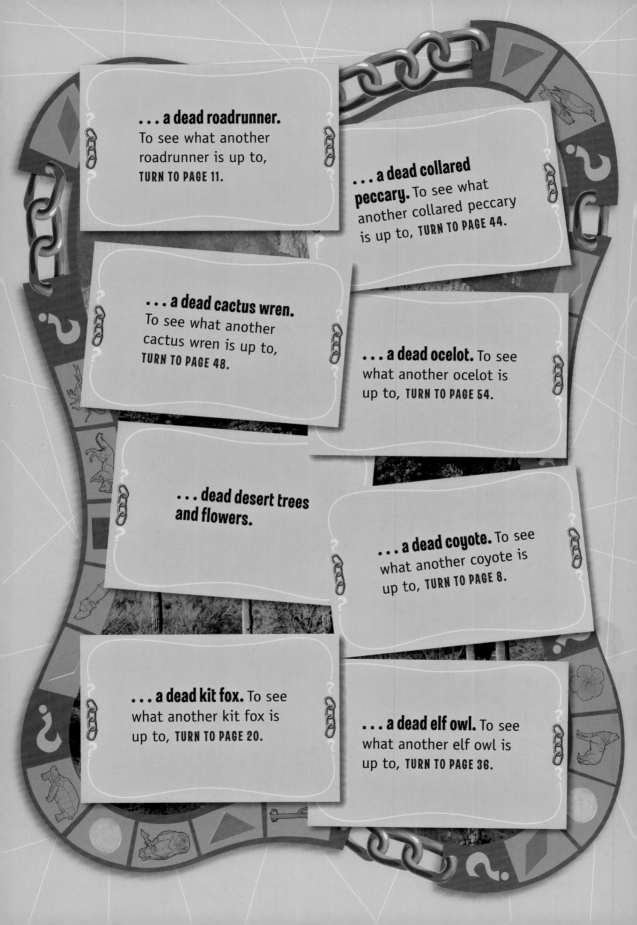

. . . a dead roadrunner. To see what another roadrunner is up to, **TURN TO PAGE 11.**

. . . a dead collared peccary. To see what another collared peccary is up to, **TURN TO PAGE 44.**

. . . a dead cactus wren. To see what another cactus wren is up to, **TURN TO PAGE 48.**

. . . a dead ocelot. To see what another ocelot is up to, **TURN TO PAGE 54.**

. . . dead desert trees and flowers.

. . . a dead coyote. To see what another coyote is up to, **TURN TO PAGE 8.**

. . . a dead kit fox. To see what another kit fox is up to, **TURN TO PAGE 20.**

. . . a dead elf owl. To see what another elf owl is up to, **TURN TO PAGE 36.**

GLOSSARY

adapt: to change so as to better survive in an environment

bacteria: tiny living things made up of only one cell

carbon dioxide: a gas that is formed by decay and that plants use for nourishment

carnivore: an animal that eats other animals

decomposers: living things, such as insects or bacteria, that feed on dead plants and animals

endangered: an animal that is in danger of dying out

exoskeleton: a hard covering on the outside of an animal

extinct: no longer existing

food chain: a system in which energy moves from the sun to plants and to animals as each eats and is eaten

food web: many food chains linked together

habitats: areas where a plant or animal naturally lives and grows

invasive species: a plant or animal that doesn't naturally live in an area

molt: to shed skin or feathers

nutrients: substances, especially in food, that help a plant or animal survive

pollinate: to transfer pollen from one flower to another. The transferred pollen allows flowers to make seeds.

predators: animals that hunt and kill other animals for food

prey: animals that are hunted for food by other animals

primary consumers: animals that eat plants

producers: living things, such as plants, that make their own food

secondary consumers: animals and insects that eat other animals and insects

tertiary consumers: animals that eat other animals and that have few natural enemies

venom: a poison made by an animal and injected into an animal it hunts

venomous: able to deliver a poisonous bite or wound

FURTHER READING AND WEBSITES

George, Jean Craighead. *One Day in the Desert*. New York: HarperCollins, 1996. This chapter book follows a mountain lion and the animals and the people he meets during a day in the Sonoran Desert.

Guiberson, Brenda Z. *Cactus Hotel*. New York: Henry Holt, 1991. Follow the life of a mighty saguaro cactus—as well as all the creatures it provides food and shelter for.

Johnson, Rebecca L. *A Walk in the Desert*. Minneapolis: Carolrhoda, 2001. Take a "stroll" through the desert to experience the sights and sounds of the desert.

Kalman, Bobbie. *What Are Food Chains and Webs?* New York: Crabtree Publishing Company, 1998. This book gives more information on food chains and food webs and lets you play a game about food chains.

The Living Desert
http://www.livingdesert.org/games_kids/sliders/aloe/deault.asp
Here you can find coloring pages and games featuring favorite desert animals and plants.

Lynch, Wayne. *The Sonoran Desert*. Lanham, MD: NorthWord, 2009. This book takes readers along on a tour of the Sonoran Desert, with full-page photos and lots of surprising facts about desert creatures.

Sonoran Desert Kids
http://www.pima.gov/cmo/sdcp/kids/index.html
This site from Pima County, Arizona, includes games and quizzes, fact sheets, and coloring pages on the wildlife of the Sonoran Desert.

Wright-Frierson, Virginia. *A Desert Scrapbook: Dawn to Dusk in the Sonoran Desert*. New York: Aladdin, 2002. The author-illustrator shares her sketches of the sights—big and small—of the Sonoran Desert.

SELECTED BIBLIOGRAPHY

Arizona-Sonora Desert Museum. 2007. http://desertmuseum.org (July 24, 2008).

Broyles, Bill. *Our Sonoran Desert.* Tucson, AZ: Rio Nuevo Publishers, 2003.

Burnie, David. *Animal: The Definitive Visual Guide to the World's Wildlife.* New York: DK, 2005.

Desert USA. *Desert USA.com.* 2008. http://www.desertusa.com (July 24, 2008).

Forest Guardian. "Deserts and Grasslands." *Forest Guardians.* June 30, 2008. http://www.fguardians.org/dg/index.asp (July 24, 2008).

National Geographic Society. *Sonoran Desert: A Violent Eden.* VHS. Washington, DC: National Geographic Video, 1997.

Olin, George. *House in the Sun: A Natural History of the Sonoran Desert.* Tucson, AZ: Southwest Parks and Monuments Association, 1994.

Spencer, Guy J. *A Living Desert.* Mahwah, NJ: Troll Associates, 1988.

U.S. Fish & Wildlife Service. "USFWS Threatened and Endangered Species System (TESS)." *FWS Endangered Species.* N.d. http://ecos.fws.gov/tess_public/StartTESS.do (July 24, 2008).

World Wildlife Fund. "Sonoran Desert." *worldwildlife.org.* 2001. http://www.worldwildlife.org/wildworld/profiles/terrestrial/na/na1310_full.html (July 24, 2008).

INDEX

Photo Acknowledgments

The images in this book are used with the permission of: © C. McIntyre/ PhotoLink/Photodisc/Getty Images, pp. 1, 4–5, 6–7, all sidebar backgrounds; © Bill Hauser/Independent Picture Service, pp. 5, 58 (bottom); © Jeff Foott/ Discovery Channel Images/Getty Images, pp. 8 (top), 9, 46 (top); © Konrad Wothe/Minden Pictures/Getty Images, p. 8 (bottom); © Arthur Morris/Visuals Unlimited, p. 11; © age fotostock/SuperStock, pp. 12, 24 (top), 32, 35, 48, 52; © Gerald & Buff Corsi/Visuals Unlimited, p. 14; © Barry Mansell/SuperStock, p. 16; © Joanna B. Pinneo/Aurora/Getty Images, p. 17; © John Cancalosi/Peter Arnold, Inc., p. 19; U.S. Fish and Wildlife Service, p. 20; © Malcolm Schuyl/ Alamy, p. 22; © Craig K. Lorenz/Photo Researchers, Inc., pp. 24 (bottom), 36 (bottom); © Tom Walker/Photographer's Choice/Getty Images, p. 26; © Joel Sartore/National Geographic/Getty Images, p. 27; © Gregory G. Dimijian, M.D./ Photo Researchers, Inc., p. 28; © Dwight R. Kuhn, p. 30; © James Randklev/ Photographer's Choice RF/Getty Images, pp. 33, 58 (top); © Anthony Mercieca/ SuperStock, p. 36 (top); © Jack Milchanowski/Visuals Unlimited, pp. 38, 40; © Dr. Merlin D. Tuttle/Photo Researchers, Inc., p. 39; © Tom Vezo/Minden Pictures/Getty Images, p. 42; © TUNS/Peter Arnold, Inc., p. 44; © Marli Miller/ Visuals Unlimited, p. 46 (bottom); © Michael & Patricia Fogden/Minden Pictures/Getty Images, p. 50; © Robert E. Barber/Alamy, p. 54; © Larry Minden/Minden Pictures/Getty Images, p. 55; © Kevin Ebi/Alamy, p. 56; © Joe McDonald/Visuals Unlimited, p. 58 (middle).

Front Cover: © C. McIntyre/PhotoLink/Photodisc/Getty Images (background); © iStockphoto.com/Anton Foltin (left); © Jeff Foott/Discovery Channel Images/ Getty Images (second from left); © Rinusbaak/Dreamstime.com (second from right); © Arthur Morris/Visuals Unlimited/Getty Images (right).

About the Authors

Don and Becky Wojahn are school library media specialists by day and writers by night. Their natural habitat is the temperate forests of northwestern Wisconsin, where they share their den with two animal-loving sons and two big black dogs. The Wojahns' other Follow that Food Chain books include *A Rain Forest Food Chain*, *A Savanna Food Chain*, *A Temperate Forest Food Chain*, *A Tundra Food Chain*, and *An Australian Outback Food Chain*.